The Speller's Bag

and other poems

Compiled by

John Foster

OXFORD
UNIVERSITY PRESS

Great Clarendon Street, Oxford OX2 6DP

Oxford University Press is a department of the University of Oxford.
It furthers the University's objective of excellence in research, scholarship,
and education by publishing worldwide in

Oxford New York
Athens Auckland Bangkok Bogotá Buenos Aires Calcutta
Cape Town Chennai Dar es Salaam Delhi Florence Hong Kong Istanbul
Karachi Kuala Lumpur Madrid Melbourne Mexico City Mumbai
Nairobi Paris São Paulo Shanghai Singapore Taipei Tokyo Toronto Warsaw

and associated companies in Berlin Ibadan

Oxford is a trade mark of Oxford University Press
in the UK and in certain other countries

© Oxford University Press 2000
First published 2000

British Library Cataloguing in Publication Data
Data available

ISBN 0 19 917363 X

Printed in Hong Kong

The National Literacy Strategy termly requirements for poetry at
Year 5 are fulfilled on the following pages:

Term 1

pp 5–11, 14–16, 26–27, 47, 56, 60, 70, 84, 86.

Term 2

pp 22, 44, 48, 50, 62, 64, 68, 72, 76, 79.

Term 3

pp 12–13, 18, 20, 24, 25, 28, 30–32, 34–35, 36, 38, 52, 54, 61,
71, 73–74, 85, 88, 90, 92.

For more detailed information on the poetry range requirements
and the termly objectives, see Oxford Literacy Web Poetry
Teacher's Guide 2.

Contents

Instructions for Growing Poetry

(found on the back of the packet)

Shut your eyes.
Open your mind.
Look inside.
What do you find?
Something funny?
Something sad?
Something beautiful,
mysterious, mad?
Open your ears.
Listen well.
A word or phrase
begins to swell?
Catch its rhythm.
Hold its sound.
Gently, slowly
roll it round.
Does it please you?
Does it tease you?
Does it ask
to grow and spread?
Now those little
words are sprouting
poetry
inside your head.

Tony Mitton

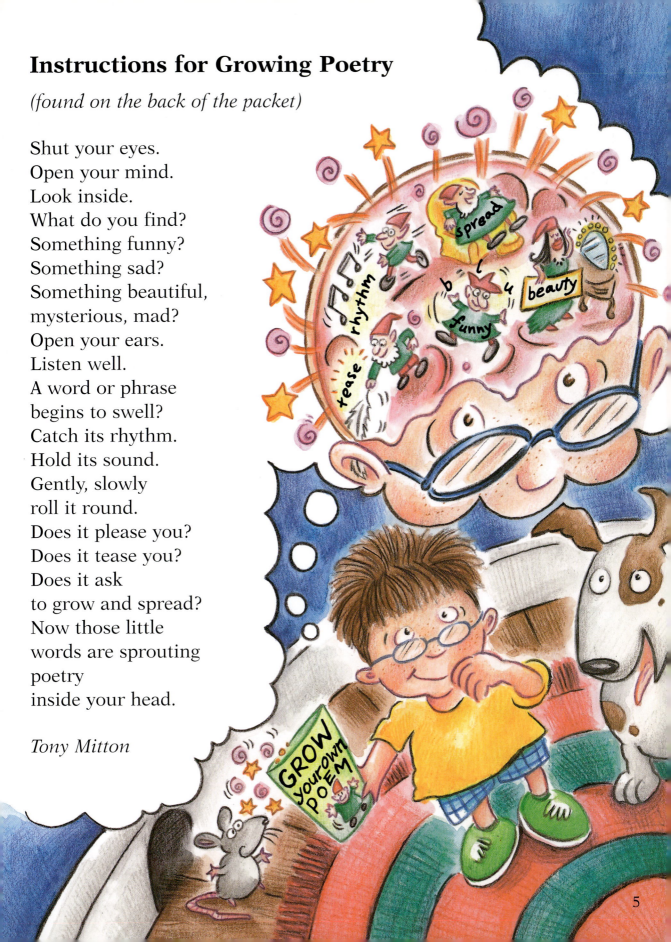

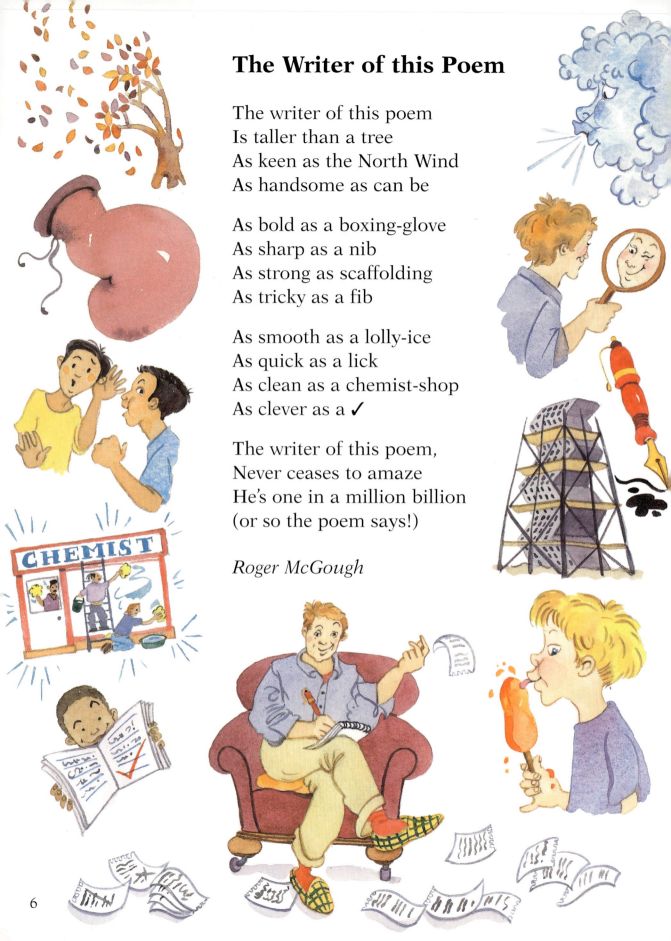

The Writer of this Poem

The writer of this poem
Is taller than a tree
As keen as the North Wind
As handsome as can be

As bold as a boxing-glove
As sharp as a nib
As strong as scaffolding
As tricky as a fib

As smooth as a lolly-ice
As quick as a lick
As clean as a chemist-shop
As clever as a ✓

The writer of this poem,
Never ceases to amaze
He's one in a million billion
(or so the poem says!)

Roger McGough

The Poet's Pen

I'm a hunter with a pen
and I'm tracking down words.

Some stay high as birds
Some keep low as worms.

But I'm armed with my pen
and I'll track words to their den.

Some words are snakes
I hear their hiss.

Some words are tigers
I hear their roar.

Some words are scorpions
Watch out for their sting.

But I'm hiding with my pen
and I'll catch them in a wink.

My God, I've run out of ink!

John Agard

Listen

Silence is when you can hear things.
Listen:
The breathing of bees,
A moth's foot fall,
Or the mist easing its way
Across the field,
The light shifting at dawn
Or the stars clicking into place
At evening.

John Cotton

Quiet Secret

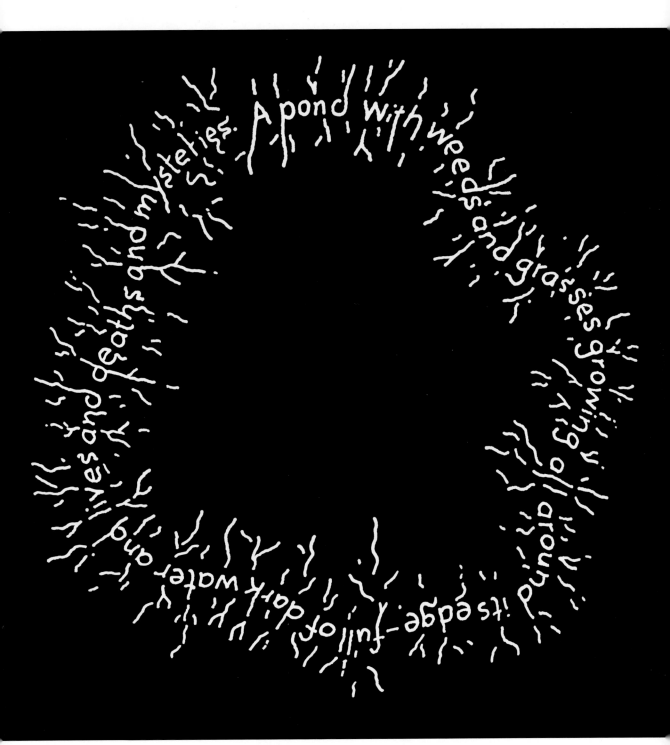

Robert Froman

Dragonflies

They used to fly
over all the ponds
in summer, granny says,

like sparkling sapphire helicopters,
purple aeroplanes,
with eyes of bright topaz,
wings flashing emerald light,
brightening the countryside
in their jewelled flight.

Sun-glow brilliance winging
over every pond,
someday I hope to see one
– smallest last dragon.

Joan Poulson

Frogspawn

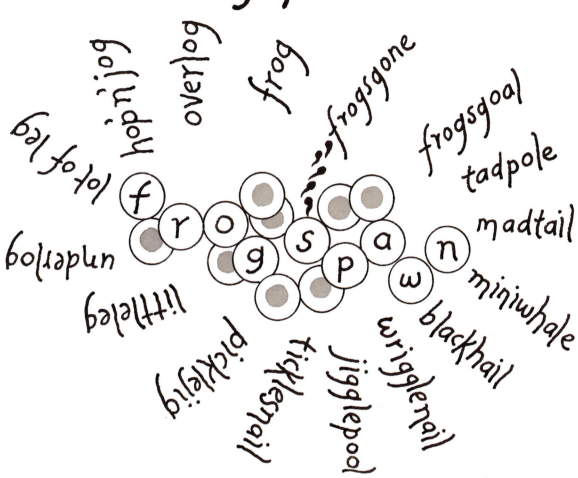

frog
overfrog
hopifrog
lot of frog
underfrog
littlefrog
picklefrog
ticklesnail
jigglepool
wrigglenail
blackhail
miniwhale
madtail
tadpole
frogsgoal
frogsgone

Judith Nicholls

Spider

spinning link

stuck in sinks

spindle legs

a thousand egg

spying eyes

trapping flie

spider

spider

Spiders!

Trevor Millum

Again Again Again Again

The spider in his crystal maze
plots and plucks his airy ways.

His web looks like a window-pane
hit by a stone, a star of rain.

A knitted net, spun silk and dew
that lets the April breeze pass through.

It glitters in the morning sun.
His work, it seems, is never done

because some stupid fly or bee
keeps smashing its frail jewellery.

And that's why, all elbows, he
swings like a yo-yo from a tree

or mends his shattered window-pane
with patient artistry again

Again, again, again, again,
again, again, again, again.

James Kirkup

The Speller's Bag

Here a bone.
Here a stone.
In my bag
I keep them all.

A stone brought me
by the sea.
A bone taken from where
I'll never tell thee.

A bone, a stone,
a feather, a shell,
all in my bag
to cast a spell.

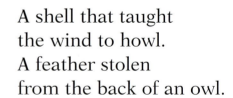

A shell that taught
the wind to howl.
A feather stolen
from the back of an owl.

Then again it might be
from a raven's neck.
I'll never tell thee.

Look inside all who dare.

Inside my bag
you'll find your fear.

John Agard

Fairy Story

I went into the wood one day
And there I walked and lost my way

When it was so dark I could not see
A little creature came to me

He said if I would sing a song
The time would not be very long

But first I must let him hold my hand tight
Or else the wood would give me a fright

I sang a song, he let me go
But now I am home again there is nobody I know.

Stevie Smith

The Dare

Go on, I dare you,
Come on down!

Was it *me* they called?
Pretend you haven't heard,
a voice commanded in my mind.
Walk past, walk fast
and don't look down,
don't look behind.

Come on, it's easy!

The banks were steep,
the water low
and flanked with oozing brown.
Easy? Walk fast
but don't look down.
Walk straight, walk on,
even risk their jeers
and run …

Never go near those dykes,
my mother said
No need to tell me.
I'd seen stones sucked in
and covered without trace,
gulls slide to bobbing safety,
grasses drown as water rose.
No need to tell me
to avoid the place.

She ca-a-a-n't, she ca-a-a-n't!
Cowardy, cowardy custard!

There's no such word as 'can't',
My father said.
I slowed my pace.
The voices stopped,
waited as I wavered, grasping breath.
My mother's wrath? My father's scorn?
A watery death?

I hesitated then turned back,
forced myself to see the mud below.
After all, it was a dare …
There was no choice;
I had to go.

Judith Nicholls

What's That Down There?

What's that down there?
What's that moving?
What's that moving down in the dark
   of this chilly black maze of a cave?

Is it Sarallo –
The scarlet snake with the seven
Silver heads
And fangs that snap like a murder trap?

What's that down there?
What's that moving?
What's that moving down in the dark
   of this chilly black maze of a cave?

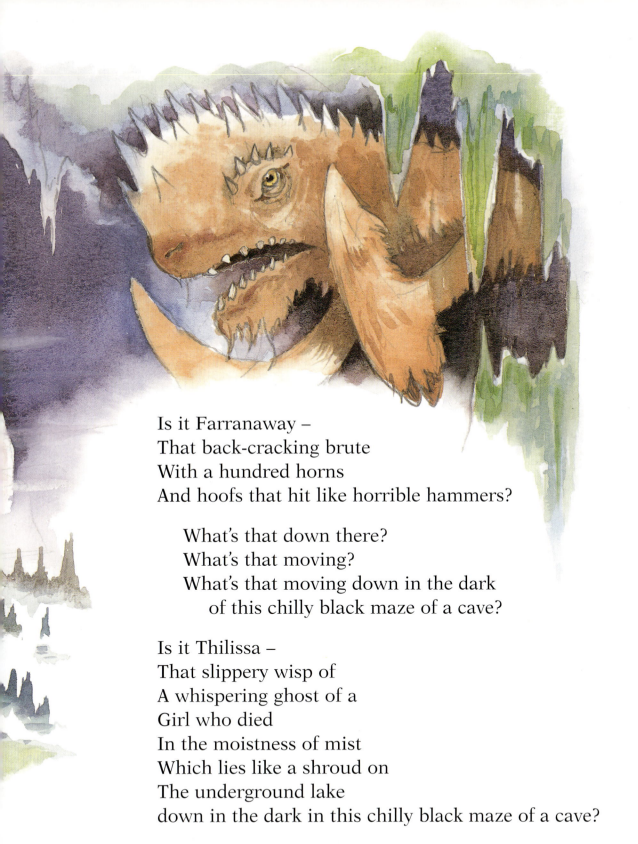

Is it Farranaway –
That back-cracking brute
With a hundred horns
And hoofs that hit like horrible hammers?

What's that down there?
What's that moving?
What's that moving down in the dark
    of this chilly black maze of a cave?

Is it Thilissa –
That slippery wisp of
A whispering ghost of a
Girl who died
In the moistness of mist
Which lies like a shroud on
The underground lake
down in the dark in this chilly black maze of a cave?

Adrian Mitchell

The Spectre on the Moor

In the ghastly, ghostly silence
of the misty misty moor,
a phosphorescent spectre
sets upon its twilight tour
searching for some hapless victim –
it will find one, oh be sure.

It swirls about the vapours
of the luminescent mist
with its tendrils slowly writhing,
deadly purpose in each twist,
and its grasp is cold and final,
not a creature can resist.

Do not go there in the twilight,
do not heed its dread allure.
It will hold you and enfold you
in such ways you can't endure,
till you never leave the spectre
on the misty misty moor.

Jack Prelutsky

The Listeners

'Is there anybody there?' said the Traveller,
    Knocking on the moonlit door;
And his horse in the silence champed the grasses
    Of the forest's ferny floor:
And a bird flew up out of the turret,
    Above the Traveller's head:
And he smote upon the door again a second time;
    'Is there anybody there?' he said,
But no one descended to the Traveller;
    No head from the leaf-fringed sill
Leaned over and looked into his grey eyes,
    Where he stood perplexed and still.
But only a host of phantom listeners
    That dwelt in the lone house then
Stood listening in the quiet of the moonlight
    To that voice from the world of men:
Stood thronging the faint moonbeams on the dark stair,
    That goes down to the empty hall,
Harkening in an air stirred and shaken
    By the lonely Traveller's call.

And he felt in his heart their strangeness,
    Their stillness answering his cry,
While his horse moved, cropping the dark turf,
    'Neath the starred and leafy sky;
For he suddenly smote on the door, even
    Louder, and lifted his head:
'Tell them I came, and no one answered,
    That I kept my word,' he said.
Never the least stir made the listeners,
    Though every word he spake
Fell echoing through the shadowiness of the still house
    From the one man left awake:
Ay, they heard his foot upon the stirrup,
    And the sound of iron on stone,
And how the silence surged softly backward,
    When the plunging hoofs were gone.

Walter de la Mare

Me and Amanda

Me
and
Amanda
meander,
like
rivers
that
run
to
the
sea.
We
wander
at
random
we're
always
in
tandem:
meandering
Mandy
and
me.

Colin West

24

Seeing Stars

the sky's not dressed
without a star
on a silver tree
a star blooms
a star is Christmas
all year round
a star's a magic
wand at rest
stars are not cold
and dead for me

Sue Cowling

Man on Moon

Stanley Cook

Pylons

Like
t
a
l
l   t h i n
ladies
they stride hand-in-hand
across the valley
their
c   e
r   a
y   r
s   r
t   i
a   n
l   g
         s
winking
elegantly
all urban sophistication
i
n
t
h
e
   y   l
   l   i
   r   g
   a   h
   e   t

Moira Andrew

27

The Song of Tyrannosaurus Rex

I'm a rock, I'm a mountain, I'm a hammer and a nail
I'm an army and a navy, I'm a force ten gale

I'm a trooper, I'm a tearaway, and time will never see
Another king, or anything, that fights like me

I'm a sinner, I'm a winner, I'm a one-man government
I'm the will of the people, I'm the force that's never spent

I'm a business and a factory, the work-force and the boss
I'm the brains and the belly and I never make a loss

I'm a monumental mason and the gravestones that I make
Are carved of flesh and bone from the carcasses I take

I'm a god, I'm a ghost, I'm the creak on the stairs
I'm the grin that listens in when people say their prayers

I'm a crane, I'm a lorry, I'm a brand-new motorway
I set like concrete and I'm here to stay

O I'm big and I'm bad and I'm bold and I'm free
And the world will never see another villain like me

For I swagger and I swallow and the earth is my hotel
And I chew my meat in heaven, and I lash my tail in hell!

William Scammell

Jocelyn, my Dragon

My dragon's name is Jocelyn,
He's something of a joke.
For Jocelyn is very tame,
He doesn't like to maul or maim,
Or breathe a fearsome fiery flame;
He's much too smart to smoke.

And when I take him to the park
The children form a queue,
And say, 'What lovely eyes of red!'
As one by one they pat his head.
And Jocelyn is so well bred,
He only eats a few!

Colin West

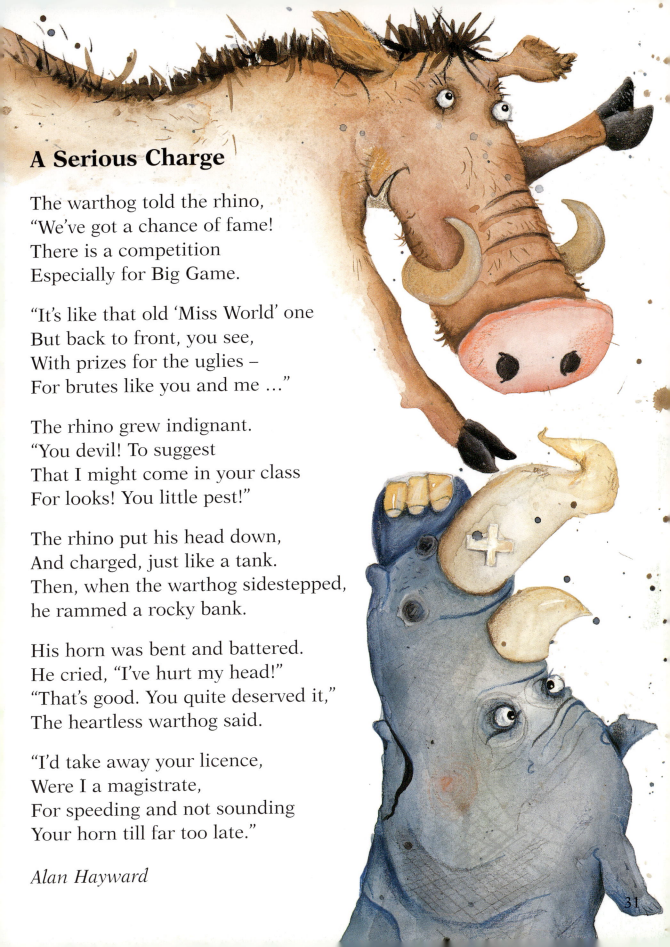

A Serious Charge

The warthog told the rhino,
"We've got a chance of fame!
There is a competition
Especially for Big Game.

"It's like that old 'Miss World' one
But back to front, you see,
With prizes for the uglies –
For brutes like you and me …"

The rhino grew indignant.
"You devil! To suggest
That I might come in your class
For looks! You little pest!"

The rhino put his head down,
And charged, just like a tank.
Then, when the warthog sidestepped,
he rammed a rocky bank.

His horn was bent and battered.
He cried, "I've hurt my head!"
"That's good. You quite deserved it,"
The heartless warthog said.

"I'd take away your licence,
Were I a magistrate,
For speeding and not sounding
Your horn till far too late."

Alan Hayward

31

The Lion and the Echo

The King of the Beasts, deep in the wood,
Roared as loudly as it could.
Right away the echo came back
And the lion thought itself under attack.

"What voice is it that roars like mine?"
The echo replied, "Mine, mine."

"Who might you be?" asked the furious lion,
"I'm King of this jungle, this jungle is mine."
And the echo came back a second time,
"This jungle is mine, is mine, is mine."

The lion swore revenge if only it could
Discover the intruder in the wood.
It roared, "Coward! Come out and show yourself!"
But the fearless echo replied simply "… elf."

"Come out," roared the lion, "enough deceit,
Do you fear for your own defeat?"
But all the echo did was repeat
"Defeat … defeat …"

Frightened by every conceivable sound,
The exhausted lion sank to the ground.
A bird in a tree looked down and it said,
"Dear lion, I'm afraid that what you hear
Is simply the voice of your lion-sized fear."

Brian Patten

The Snake Song

Neither legs nor arms have I
But I crawl on my belly
And I have
Venom, venom, venom!

Neither horns nor hoofs have I
But I spit with my tongue
And I have
Venom, venom, venom!

Neither bows nor guns have I
But I flash fast with my tongue
And I have
Venom, venom, venom!

Neither radar nor missiles have I
But I stare with my eyes
And I have
Venom, venom, venom!

I master every movement
For I jump, run and swim
And I spit
Venom, venom, venom!

John Mbiti

Camel's Invitation

Touch my hump
and the desert
will linger on your hands

Look into
the good book of my eyes
and you will see a star
in the east
where the wise ones sit

Cradle the beast
that kneels on sand
and you will feel
such a beautiful thirst

From this day on
you will walk with your lips
to the sky

John Agard

The Magnificent Bull

My bull is white like the silver fish in the river
white like the shimmering crane bird on the river bank
white like fresh milk!
His roar is like the thunder to the Turkish
      cannon on the steep shore.
My bull is dark like the raincloud in the storm.
He is like summer and winter.
Half of him is dark like the storm cloud,
half of him is light like sunshine.
His back shines like the morning star.
His brow is red like the beak of the Hornbill.
His forehead is like a flag, calling the people from a distance,
He resembles the rainbow.

I will water him at the river,
With my spear I shall drive my enemies.
Let them water their herds at the well;
the river belongs to me and my bull.
Drink, my bull, from the river; I am here
to guard you with my spear.

Ulli Beier

Don' Go Ova Dere

Barry madda tell im
But Barry wouldn't hear,
Barry fada warn im
But Barry didn' care.
'Don' go ova dere, bwoy,
Don' go ova dere.'

Barry sista beg im
Barry pull her hair,
Barry brother bet im
'You can't go ova dere.'
'I can go ova dere, bwoy,
I can go ova dere.'

Barry get a big bag,
Barry climb de gate,
Barry granny call im
But Barry couldn't wait,
Im wan' get ova dere, bwoy,
Before it get too late.

Barry see de plum tree
Im didn' see de bull,
Barry thinkin' bout de plums
'Gwine get dis big bag full'.
De bull get up an' shake, bwoy,
And gi de rope a pull.

De rope slip off de pole
But Barry didn' see,
De bull begin to stretch im foot den
Barry climb de tree.
Barry start fe eat, bwoy,
Firs' one, den two, den three.

Barry nearly full de bag
An den im hear a soun'
Barry hol' de plum limb tight
And start fe look aroun'
When im see de bull, bwoy,
Im nearly tumble down.

40

Night a come, de bull naw move,
From unda de plum tree,
Barry madda wondering
Whey Barry coulda be.
Barry getting tired, bwoy,
Of sittin' in dat tree.

An Barry dis realise
Him neva know before,
Sey de tree did full o' black ants
But now im know fe sure.
For some begin fe bite im, bwoy,
Den more, an more, an more.

De bull lay down fe wait it out,
Barry mek a jump,
De bag o' plum drop out de tree
An Barry hear a thump.
By early de nex' mawnin', bwoy,
Dat bull gwine have a lump.

De plum so frighten dat po' bull
Im start fe run too late,
Im a gallop afta Barry
But Barry jump de gate.
De bull jus' stamp im foot, bwoy,
Im yeye dem full o' hate.

When Barry ketch a im yard,
What a state im in!
Im los' im bag, im clothes mud up,
An mud deh pon im chin.
An whey de black ants bite im
Feba bull-frog skin.

Barry fada spank im,
Im madda sey im sin,
Barry sista scold im
But Barry only grin,
For Barry brother shake im head
An sey, 'Barry, yuh win!'

Valerie Bloom

43

Growing Pains

The twelfth of August,
The sun-baked ground brown concrete,
the yellow grass sparse hair
on an old woman's head,

ants like freckles
twitch between the thin wisps;
everybody lies and gasps
except my father.

Swollen with energy he capers,
bulgy over crimson boxer shorts;
I cringe behind the apple tree –
how stupid he looks.

How childish he is:
How could he:
what if someone sees him
dressed like that –

gamboling like a loon
all flab and chest hair,
long short grey socks,
and rubber flip-flops?

Then Dad lifts the rabbit from its run
and trots around the garden,
the big black buck held firm
against his naked chest,

giving it a guided tour – 'These are
the cabbages – yum – yum – and there, the goozygogs...'
My Mum, flat out beneath a William Pear
sees danger: 'Do be careful, dear.

45

If Sooty jumps – you know how strong
his back legs are.' My Dad
stares into the rabbit's eyes:
'He wouldn't hurt his Daddy,
would he?'

The rabbit, bored of being Bunny,
leaps free. Kicking back
his claws leave four great
bleeding weals across my father's chest.

My mother crows – 'I told you so'
and leads the way in doors to
bathe the wounds in antiseptic.
Me – so much more adult,

embarrassed, bored and cross
beneath the tree –
'Serves him right, serves him right,
serves him right!'

From somewhere in the house
I hear a bellow
as the antiseptic stings:
'Big Baby!'

Mick Gowar

46

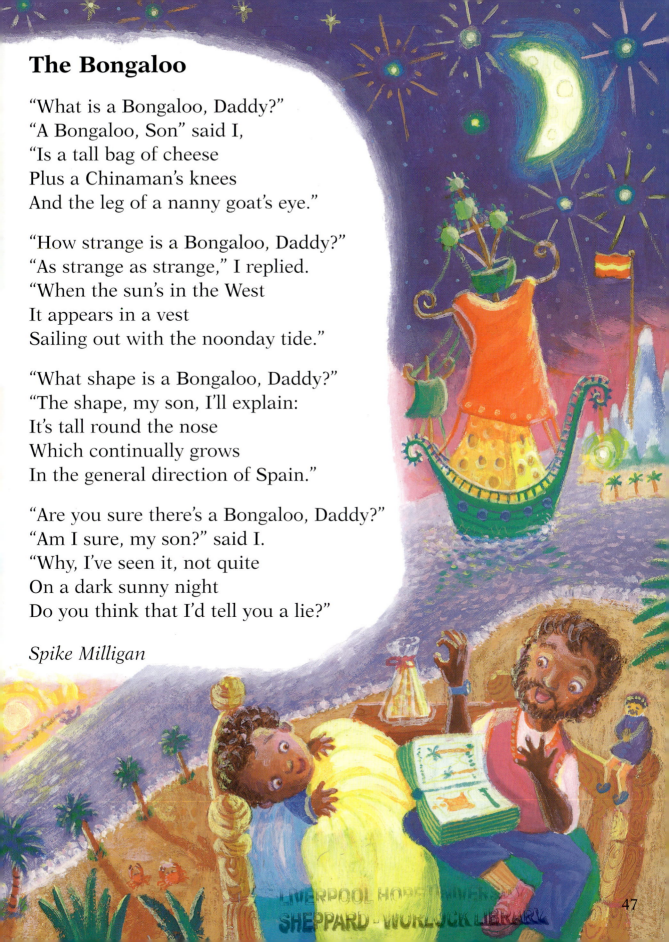

The Bongaloo

"What is a Bongaloo, Daddy?"
"A Bongaloo, Son" said I,
"Is a tall bag of cheese
Plus a Chinaman's knees
And the leg of a nanny goat's eye."

"How strange is a Bongaloo, Daddy?"
"As strange as strange," I replied.
"When the sun's in the West
It appears in a vest
Sailing out with the noonday tide."

"What shape is a Bongaloo, Daddy?"
"The shape, my son, I'll explain:
It's tall round the nose
Which continually grows
In the general direction of Spain."

"Are you sure there's a Bongaloo, Daddy?"
"Am I sure, my son?" said I.
"Why, I've seen it, not quite
On a dark sunny night
Do you think that I'd tell you a lie?"

Spike Milligan

Father William

"You are old, Father William," the young man said,
    "And your hair has become very white;
And yet you incessantly stand on your head –
    Do you think, at your age, it is right?"

"In my youth," Father William replied to his son,
    "I feared it might injure my brain;
But, now that I'm perfectly sure I have none,
    Why, I do it again and again."

"You are old," said the youth, "as I mentioned before,
    And have grown most uncommonly fat;
Yet you turned a back-somersault in at the door –
    Pray, what is the reason of that?"

"In my youth," said the sage, as he shook his gray locks,
    "I kept all my limbs very supple
By the use of this ointment – one shilling the box –
    Allow me to sell you a couple?"

"You are old," said the youth, "and your jaws are too weak
    For anything tougher than suet;
Yet you finished the goose, with the bones and the beak –
    Pray, how did you manage to do it?"

"In my youth," said his father, "I took to the law,
    And argued each case with my wife;
And the muscular strength which it gave to my jaw
    Has lasted the rest of my life."

"You are old," said the youth, "one would hardly suppose
    That your eye was as steady as ever;
Yet you balanced an eel on the end of your nose –
    What made you so awfully clever?"

"I have answered three questions, and that is enough,"
    Said his father; "don't give yourself airs!
Do you think I can listen all day to such stuff?
    Be off, or I'll kick you downstairs!"

Lewis Carroll

A Tragic Story

There lived a sage in days of yore,
And he a handsome pigtail wore:
But wondered much, and sorrowed more,
    Because it hung behind him.

He mused upon this curious case,
And swore he'd change the pigtail's place,
And have it hanging at his face,
    Not dangling there behind him.

Says he, "The mystery I've found –
I'll turn me round," – he turned him round,
    But still it hung behind him.

Then round, and round, and out and in,
All day the puzzled sage did spin;
In vain – it mattered not a pin –
    The pigtail hung behind him.

And right and left, and round about,
And up and down, and in and out,
He turned; but still the pigtail stout
   Hung steadily behind him.

And though his efforts never slack,
And though he twist, and twirl, and tack,
Alas! Still faithful to his back,
   The pigtail hangs behind him.

William Makepeace Thackeray

51

The Guzzler

Mr Guzzledy-Gulpity-Gobbly McGhee
(Known as Mac) has a craving to drink cups of tea.
He'll drink ten in the morning, ten more before bed,
And another ten cups in the night, I've heard said.

In his youth he was normal, then something went wrong.
When in hospital, Mac (who had stayed there too long)
Had a tired little nurse who made such a bad slip
That she plugged in a flask of cold tea to his drip.

When she saw what she'd done, she cried out, "Oh, dear me!
Oh, that poor man's transfusion's not blood, it is tea!"
Then she screamed, "Doctor! Doctor!" – an earsplitting shout.
But he said, "You're too late, for I can't take it out."

Thus, the tea that went into Mac's veins on that day
Is there still, for it clings and it won't go away.
So old Guzzledy Mac has got tea in his blood
Which explains why he drinks such an unending flood.

Alan Hayward

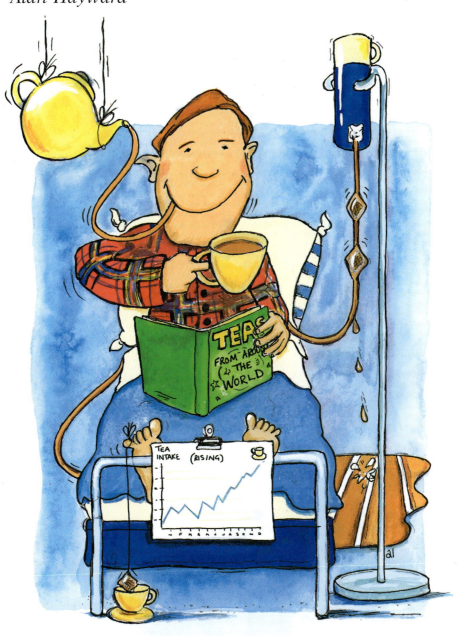

The Punishment

I had a dreadful nightmare
I dreamt I was my dad
I took away my privileges
Because I had been bad.

I sent myself up to my room
And locked myself inside
Then sat there knotted up with guilt
As I broke down and cried.

We were both extremely sorry
But both too proud to speak
So this miserable punishment
Went on another week.

I told myself: "Give me a break!"
I yelled, "Give me one too!"
We wound ourselves into a knot
Which no one could undo.

When I woke in the morning
And was myself once more
I thought that sulking half my life
Could start to be a chore.

I made a resolution
I promised to be good
Of course I didn't stick to it
D'you really think I would?

So now when dad is mad with me
I take it on the chin
For though the punishment's hard on me
It's just as hard on him.

Lindsay Macrae

55

The Car Trip

Mum says:
"Right, you two,
this is a very long car journey.
I want you two to be good.
I'm driving and I can't drive properly
if you two are going mad in the back.
Do you understand?"

So we say,
"OK, Mum, OK. Don't worry,"
and off we go.

And we start The Moaning:
Can I have a drink?
I want some crisps.
Can I open my window?
He's got my book.
Get off me.
Ow, that's my ear!

And Mum tries to be exciting:
"Look out the window
there's a lamp post."

And we go on with The Moaning:
Can I have a sweet?
He's sitting on me.
Are we nearly there?
Don't scratch.
You never tell him off.
Now he's biting his nails.
I want a drink. I want a drink.

And Mum tries to be exciting again:
"Look out the window
There's a tree."

And we go on:
My hands are sticky
He's playing with the doorhandle now.
I feel sick.
Your nose is all runny.
Don't pull my hair.

He's punching me, Mum,
That's really dangerous, you know.
Mum, he's spitting.

And Mum says:
"Right I'm stopping the car.
I AM STOPPING THE CAR."

She stops the car.

"Now, if you two don't stop it
I'm going to put you out the car
And leave you by the side of the road."

He started it.
I didn't. He started it.

"I don't care who started it
I can't drive properly
If you two go mad in the back.
Do you understand?"

And we say:
OK, Mum, OK, don't worry.

Can I have a drink?

Michael Rosen

Teacher's Prayer

Let the children in our care
Clean their shoes and comb their hair;
Come to school on time – and neat
Blow their noses, wipe their feet.
Let them, Lord *not* eat in class
Or rush into the hall en masse.
Let them show some self-control;
Let them slow down; let them *stroll*!

Let the children in our charge
Not be violent or large;
Not be sick on the school-trip bus,
Not be cleverer than *us*;
Not be unwashed, loud or mad,
(With a six-foot mother or a seven-foot dad).
Let them please say "drew" not "drawed";
Let them know the *answers*, Lord!

Allan Ahlberg

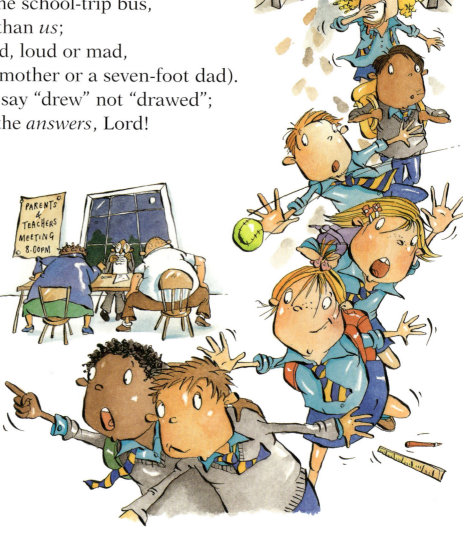

Who Killed the Swan?

Who killed the swan?
'I,' said the weight,
'My poison lead she ate,
I killed the swan.'

Who left it there?
'I,' said the fisherman,
'When my day was done
I left it there.'

Who saw her die?
'We,' said the reeds,
'She fell amongst our leaves.
We saw her die.'

Who will mourn her passing?
'I,' said the water,
'For she was my daughter.
I will mourn her passing.'

Edward Turnbull

Saint Christopher

'Carry me Ferryman, over the ford.'
'My boat is my back little boy. Come aboard.
Some men have muscle, and some men have mind,
And my strength is my gift for the good of mankind.'

'Shall I not weigh on you crossing the ford?'
'I've carried a king and his crown and his sword,
A labourer too with his spade and his plough.
What's a mere child to me? Come along now.'

'Ferryman why do you pant at the ford?'
'My muscles are iron, my sinews are cord,
But my back with your burden is ready to break,
You double your weight, child, with each step I take!'

'Ferryman, bearer of men o'er the ford,
Christopher, Christopher, I am your Lord.
My frame may be little, and slender my girth,
But they hold all the sorrows and sins of the earth.

'You have borne the whole world on your back through the ford,
You have carried a King and His crown and His sword,
A Labourer too with His spade and His plough,
And in one Child all little ones. Put me down now.'

Christopher set the Child down on the sward,
Christopher fell on his face by the ford.
He heard a voice uttering, 'Keep me in mind!
Our strength is our gift for the good of mankind.'

Eleanor Farjeon

Lord Ullin's Daughter

A chieftain to the Highlands bound
Cries, "Boatman, do not tarry!
And I'll give thee a silver pound
To row us o'er the ferry!"

"Now who be ye, would cross Loch Gyle,
This dark and stormy water?"
"O I'm the chief of Ulva's Isle,
And this, Lord Ullin's daughter.

"And fast before her father's men
Three days we've fled together,
For should he find us in the glen,
My blood would stain the heather.

His horsemen hard behind us ride –
Should they our steps discover,
Then who will cheer my bonny bride
When they have slain her lover?"

Out spoke the hardy Highland wight,
"I'll go, my chief, I'm ready:
It is not for your silver bright,
But for your winsome lady –

"And, by my word, the bonny bird
In danger shall not tarry;
So though the waves are raging white,
I'll row you o'er the ferry."

By this the storm grew loud apace,
The water-wraith was shrieking;
And in scowl of heaven each face
Grew dark as they were speaking.

But still as wilder blew the wind,
And as the night grew drearer,
Adown the glen rode arméd men,
Their trampling sounded nearer.

"O haste thee, haste!" the lady cries,
"Though tempests round us gather;
I'll meet the raging of the skies,
But not an angry father."

The boat has left a stormy land,
A stormy sea before her –
When O! too strong for human hand
The tempest gathered o'er her.

And still they rowed amidst the roar
Of waters fast prevailing:
Lord Ullin reached that fatal shore –
His wrath was changed to wailing.

For, sore dismayed, through storm and shade
His child he did discover;
One lovely hand she stretched for aid,
And one was round her lover.

"Come back! Come back!" he cried in grief,
"Across this stormy water,
And I'll forgive your Highland chief,
My daughter! – O, my daughter!"

'Twas vain: the loud waves lashed the shore,
Return or aid preventing;
The waters wild went o'er his child,
And he was left lamenting.

Thomas Campbell

The Visitor

A crumbling churchyard, the sea and the moon;
The waves had gouged out grave and bone;
A man was walking, late and alone …

He saw a skeleton on the ground;
A ring on a bony finger he found.

He ran home to his wife and gave her the ring.
"Oh, where did you get it?" He said not a thing.

"It's the loveliest ring in the world," she said,
As it glowed on her finger. They slipped off to bed.

At midnight they woke. In the dark outside,
"Give me my ring!" a chill voice cried.

"What was that William? What did it say?"
"Don't worry, my dear. It'll soon go away."

"I'm coming!" A skeleton opened the door.
"Give me my ring!" It was crossing the floor.

"What was that, William? What did it say?"
"Don't worry, my dear. It'll soon go away."

"I'm reaching you now! I'm climbing the bed."
The wife pulled the sheet right over her head.

It was torn from her grasp and tossed in the air:
"I'll drag you out of bed by the hair!"

"What was that William? What did it say?"
"Throw the ring through the window! THROW IT AWAY!"

She threw it. The skeleton leapt from the sill,
Scooped up the ring and clattered downhill,
Fainter … and fainter … Then all was still.

Ian Serraillier

Haiku for Autumn

Hedgerows fired with beech,
lawn smouldering with apples;
golden October!

Silence pungent as
oranges, darkened summits
humped with wind-bared rock.

Rush of water over stone
and not-quite-silences
of wind through trees.

Judith Nicholls

There is Joy

There is joy in
Feeling the warmth
Come to the great world
And seeing the sun
Follow its old footprints
In the summer night.

There is fear in
Feeling the cold
Come to the great world
And seeing the moon
– Now new moon, now full moon –
Follow its old footprints
In the winter night.

Traditional Eskimo

Winter

When icicles hang by the wall,
    And Dick the shepherd blows his nail,
And Tom bears logs into the hall,
    And milk comes frozen home in pail,
When blood is nipp'd and ways be foul,
Then nightly sings the staring owl,
                  Tu-who;
Tu-whit, tu-who – a merry note,
While greasy Joan doth keel the pot.

When all aloud the wind doth blow,
    And coughing drowns the parson's saw,
And birds sit brooding in the snow,
    And Marian's nose looks red and raw,
When roasted crabs hiss in the bowl,
Then nightly sings the staring owl,
                  Tu-who;
Tu-whit, tu-who – a merry note,
While greasy Joan doth keel the pot.

William Shakespeare

Winter

Winter crept
through the whispering wood,
hushing fir and oak;
crushed each leaf and froze each web –
but never a word he spoke.

Winter prowled
by the shivering sea,
lifting sand and stone;
nipped each limpet silently –
and then moved on.

Winter raced
down the frozen stream,
catching at his breath;
on his lips were icicles,
at his back was death.

Judith Nicholls

Over to Our Reporter on the Front Line . . .

. . . It was a surprise attack
Coming in from the south
While the city was asleep.
One by one, parks, gardens,
Streets and squares,
Were quietly taken out,
And by daybreak
It seemed all over.

But then the resistance began.
Men with trucks,
Women at their gates with brooms
Fought bravely back,
And despite reports that children
Had welcomed the invader,
In less than half a day
The enemy lay beaten
Or was driven underground
Into the drains.

All's quiet now on the streets.
I've been outside
And people are emerging
From their homes.
But as one old lady told me,
'We're not safe yet. You can never be sure.
Spring's a long way off, –
Blooming snow!'

Richard Edwards

Excelsior

The shades of night were falling fast,
As through an Alpine village passed
A youth, who bore, 'mid snow and ice,
A banner with the strange device,
   Excelsior!

His brow was sad, his eye beneath
Flashed like a faulchion from its sheath,
And like a silver clarion rung
The accents of that unknown tongue,
   Excelsior!

In happy homes he saw the light
Of household fire gleam warm and bright;
Above, the spectral glaciers shone,
And from his lips escaped a groan,
   Excelsior!

'Try not the Pass!' the old man said,
Dark lowers the tempest overhead,
The roaring torrent is deep and wide,
And loud that clarion voice replied,
    Excelsior!

'O stay!' the maiden said, 'and rest
Thy weary head upon this breast.'
A tear stood in his bright blue eye,
But still he answered with a sigh,
    Excelsior!

'Beware the pine-tree's withered branch!
Beware the awful avalanche!'
This was the peasant's last goodnight!
A voice replied, far up the height,
  Excelsior!

At break of day, as heavenward
The pious monks of Saint Bernard
Uttered the oft-repeated prayer,
A voice cried through the startled air,
  Excelsior!

A traveller, by the faithful hound,
Half-buried in the snow, was found,
Still grasping in his hand of ice
That banner, with the strange device
  Excelsior!

There, in the twilight cold and grey,
Lifeless, but beautiful, he lay
And from the sky, serene, and far,
A voice fell, like a falling star,
  Excelsior!

Henry Wadsworth Longfellow

A Legend of the Northland

Away, away in the Northland,
　　Where the hours of the day are few,
And the nights are so long in winter
　　That they cannot sleep them through;

Where they harness the swift reindeer
　　To the sledges, when it snows;
And the children look like bear's cubs
　　In their funny, furry clothes:

They tell them a curious story –
　　I don't believe 'tis true;
And yet you may learn a lesson
　　If I tell the tale to you.

Once, when the good Saint Peter
　　Lived in the world below,
And walked about it, preaching,
　　Just as he did, you know,

He came to the door of a cottage,
  In travelling round the earth,
Where a little woman was making cakes,
  And baking them on the hearth;

And being faint with fasting,
  For the day was almost done,
He asked her, from her store of cakes,
  To give him a single one.

So she made a very little cake,
  But as it baking lay,
She looked at it, and thought it seemed
  Too large to give away.

Therefore she kneaded another,
    And still a smaller one;
But it looked, when she turned it over,
    As large as the first had done.

Then she took a tiny scrap of dough,
    And rolled and rolled it flat;
And baked it thin as a wafer –
    But she couldn't part with that.

For she said, 'My cakes that seem too small
    When I eat of them myself
Are yet too large to give away.'
    So she put them on the shelf.

Then good Saint Peter grew angry,
　　For he was hungry and faint;
And surely such a woman,
　　Was enough to provoke a saint.

And he said, 'You are far too selfish
　　To dwell in a human form,
To have both food and shelter,
　　And fire to keep you warm.

'Now you shall build as the birds do,
　　And shall get your scanty food
By boring, and boring, and boring,
　　All day in the hard, dry wood.'

Then up she went through the chimney,
    Never speaking a word,
And out of the top flew a woodpecker,
    For she was changed to a bird.

She had a scarlet cap on her head,
    And that was left the same,
But all the rest of her clothes were burned
    Black as coal in the flame.

And every country schoolboy
    Has seen her in the wood,
Where she lives in the trees till this very day,
    Boring and boring for food.

Phoebe Cary

No Answer

Once the seals had skins
shiny wet as a new anorak.

Now their skins have a rusty look
of an old car part.
The star has fallen out of their eye.

The seals have no answer
to the question
of poisonous waste.

O laughter
walk on water
that the seals may smile again.

John Agard

Harvest Hymn

We plough the fields and scatter
our pesticides again:
our seeds are fed and watered
by gentle acid rain.
We spray the corn in winter
till pests and weeds are dead –
who minds a little poison
inside his daily bread?

All good gifts around us
beneath our ozone layer
are safe, oh lord,
so thank you Lord
that we know how to care.

Judith Nicholls

What on Earth?

What on earth are we doing?
Once wood-pigeons flew,
and young badgers tunnelled
where oak and ash grew ...

Now the forest's a runway,
and all that flies through
is a whining grey plane
where the pigeons once flew.

Where on earth are we going?
At the end of the lane
once blackberries hung
in soft autumn rain ...

Now the lane is a car park,
and never again
will fruit fill our baskets
down in the lane.

Why on earth are we crying?
Once morning dew shone
on hawthorn and primrose,
caught in the sun …

Now the forest is carpeted
only with stone.
No primrose, no hawthorn;
the forest has gone.

Judith Nicholls

The Recycling Rap

Listen to me children. Hear what I say.
We've got to start recycling. It's the only way
To save this planet for future generations –
The name of the game is reclamation.
You've got to start recycling. You know it makes sense.
You've got to start recyling. Stop sitting on the fence.
No more pussyfooting. No more claptrap.
Get yourself doing the recycling rap.

Come on and start recycling. Start today
By saving old newspapers, not throwing them away.
Don't just take them and dump them on the tip,
Tie them in a bundle and put them in the skip.

Get collecting, protecting the future's up to you.
Save all your old glass bottles and your jamjars too.
Take them to the bottle bank, then at the factory
The glass can be recycled, saving energy.

Don't chuck away that empty drink can.
Remember what I said. Start recycling, man.
Wash it, squash it, squeeze it flat and thin.
Take it to the Save-a-Can and post it in.

Listen to me children. Hear what I say.
We've got to start recycling. It's the only way
To save this planet for future generations –
The name of the game is reclamation.
You've got to start recycling. You know it makes sense.
You've got to start recycling. Stop sitting on the fence.
No more pussyfooting. No more claptrap.
Get yourself doing the recycling rap.

John Foster

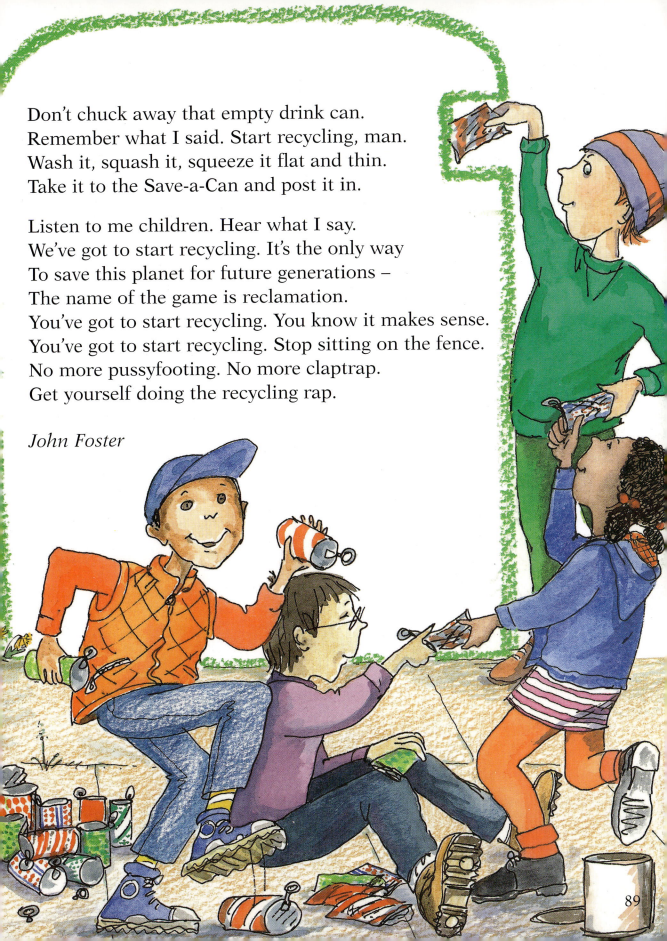

The World with its Countries

The world with its countries,
Mountains and seas,
Peoples and creatures,
Flowers and trees,
The fish in the waters,
The birds in the air
Are calling to ask us
All to take care.

These are our treasures,
A gift from above,
We should say thank you
With a care that shows love
For the blue of the ocean,
The clearness of air,
The wonder of forests
And the valleys so fair.

We should care for all people,
The rich for the poor,
Those who live in the lush lands
For those who want for
Food in the deserts,
Or are ravaged by war.
They're our sisters and brothers,
We should all love them more.

The victims of earthquakes,
The homeless through flood,
Whose farms and smallholdings
Are buried by mud,
Those bombed and fire blasted
In mindless men's wars.
Need the help of the caring
And balm for their sores.

The song of the skylark,
The warmth of the sun,
The rushing of clear streams
And new life begun
Are gifts we should cherish,
So join in the call
To strive to preserve them
For the future of all.

John Cotton

The Easterner's Prayer

I pray the prayer the Easterners do –
May the peace of Allah abide with you!
Wherever you stay wherever you go
May the beautiful palms of Allah grow,
Through days of labour and nights of rest,
The love of good Allah make you blest.
So I touch my heart as Easterners do –
May the peace of Allah abide with you!

                  Salaam Alaikum
                  (Peace be unto you)

Anon

Index of First Lines

Acknowledgements

The editor and publisher are grateful for permission to include the following poems:

John Agard: 'The Poet's Pen' and 'The Speller's Bag' from *Grandfather's Brukka Down Car* (Bodley Head, 1994), copyright © John Agard 1994, reprinted by permission of The Random House Group Ltd, and John Agard, c/o Caroline Sheldon Literary Agency; 'Camel's Invitation' from *We Animals Would Like a World with You* (Bodley Head, 1996), reprinted by permission of John Agard, c/o Caroline Sheldon Literary Agency; 'No Answer' copyright © John Agard 2000, first published in this collection by permission of the author; **Allan Ahlberg:** 'Teacher's Prayer' from *Heard it in the Playground* (Viking, 1989), copyright © Allan Ahlberg 1989, reprinted by permission of Penguin Books Ltd; **Moira Andrew:** 'Pylons', copyright © Moira Andrew 2000, first published in this collection by permission of the author; **Valerie Bloom:** 'Don't go Ova Dere' from *Duppy Jamboree* (Cambridge University Press, 1992), reprinted by permission of the author and the publisher; **Ulli Beier:** 'The Magnificent Bull' from *African Poetry* (Cambridge University Press); **Stanley Cook:** 'Man on the Moon', copyright © the estate of Stanley Cook, first published in *Spaceways* edited by John Foster (OUP, 1986), reprinted by permission of Sarah Matthews; **John Cotton:** 'Listen', first published in *The Crystal Zoo* edited by Michael Harrison (OUP, 1985); 'The World With its Countries', copyright © John Cotton 2000, first published in this collection, both reprinted by permission of the author; **Sue Cowling:** 'Seeing Stars', copyright © Sue Cowling 2000, first published in this collection by permission of the author; **Walter de la Mare:** 'The Listeners' from *The Complete Poems of Walter de la Mare* (1969), reprinted by permission of The Literary Trustees of Walter de la Mare, and the Society of Authors as their representative; **Richard Edwards:** 'Over to Our Reporter on the Front Line' from *Teaching the Parrot* (Faber), reprinted by permission of the author; **Eleanor Farjeon:** 'Saint Christopher' from *The Children's Bells*, copyright © Eleanor Farjeon 1957, reprinted by permission of David Higham Associates; **John Foster:** 'The Recycling Rap' from *Standing on the Sidelines* (OUP, 1995), copyright © John Foster 1995, reprinted by permission of the author; **Robert Froman:** 'Quiet Secret' from *Seeing Things* (Abelard-Schuman), reprinted by permission of Kate Froman; **Mick Gower:** 'Growing Pains', copyright © Mick Gower, reprinted by permission of the author; **Alan Hayward:** 'A Serious Charge' and 'The Guzzler' from *Fun Poems* (Summersdale Publishers, 1997), copyright © 1997, reprinted by permission of the author; **James Kirkup:** 'Again Again Again Again', copyright © James Kirkup, reprinted by permission of the author; **Lindsay Macrae:** 'The Punishment' from *You Canny Shove Yer Granny Off a Bus* (Viking, 1995), copyright © Lindsay Macrae 1995, reprinted by permission of Penguin Books Ltd. **Roger McGough:** 'The Writer of this Poem' from *Sky in the Pie* (Viking, 1983); **Spike Milligan:** 'The Bongaloo' from *Silly Verse for Kids* (Puffin), reprinted by permission of Spike Milligan Productions; **Trevor Millum:** 'Spider', copyright © Trevor Millum 2000, first published in this collection by permission of the author; **Adrian Mitchell:** 'What's That Down There?' from *Balloon Lagoon and the Magic Islands of Poetry* (Orchard Books, 1997), copyright © Adrian Mitchell 1997, reprinted by permission of Peters Fraser Dunlop on behalf of Adrian Mitchell. Educational Health Warning! Adrian Mitchell asks that none of his poems are used in connection with any examinations whatsoever; **Tony Mitton:** 'Instructions for Growing Poetry' from *Plum* (Scholastic Children's Books, 1998), copyright © Tony Mitton 1998, reprinted by permission of David Higham Associates; **Judith Nicholls:** 'Frogspawn', 'The Dare', 'Haiku for Autumn', 'Winter', 'Harvest Hymn' and 'What on Earth', all copyright © 2000, first published in this collection by permission of the author; **Brian Patten:** 'The Lion and the Echo' from *Gargling With Jelly* (Viking, 1985), copyright © Brian Patten 1985, reprinted by permission of Penguin Books Ltd; **Joan Poulson:** 'Dragonflies', first published in *A Glass of Fresh Air* (Collins Educational, 1996), copyright © Joan Poulson 1996, reprinted by permission of the author; **Jack Prelutsky:** 'The Spectre on the Moor' from *The Headless Horseman Rides Again* (A & C Black) **Michael Rosen:** 'The Car Trip' from *The Hypnotiser and Other Skyfoogling Poems* (Collins, 1988), reprinted by permission of the publisher and autor; **Ian Serraillier:** 'The Visitor' by permission of Anne Serraillier. **Stevie Smith:** 'Fairy Story' from *Collected Poems of Stevie Smith* (Allen Lane, 1972), reprinted by permission of The Stevie Smith Estate. **Colin West:** 'Jocelyn, My Dragon', copyright © Colin West 1982, first published in *Not To Be Taken Seriously* (Hutchinson, 1982); 'Me and Amanda', copyright © Colin West 1988, first published in *What Would You Do With a Wobble-Dee-Woo?* (Hutchinson, 1988), both reprinted by permission of the author.

Although we have tried to trace and contact copyright holders before publication, in some cases this has not been possible. If contacted we will be pleased to rectify any errors or omissions at the earliest opportunity.

The Artists

Jeff Anderson pp 64–65, 66–67;

, 94;

⌐9, 74–75;

40–41, 42–43;

⌐p 28–29, 79, 80–81, 82–83, 84–85;